Fascinating Womanhood
for the
Timeless Woman

Student Workbook

Printing Date: June 2019

Copyright 2019

By Axicon Circle, LLC

ISBN: 978-1-946032-16-4

By Dixie Andelin Forsyth

Editing, Design & Additional Content by Melissa Forsyth

Art by Shintayu Arafin and Emily Andelin Hicks

Table of Contents

Introduction by Dixie Andelin Forsyth

Section 1 – *Reclaiming Femininity*

Intro Class

Introduction

Welcome to Fascinating Womanhood for the Timeless Woman Comprehensive Course! This workbook
can be used in both self-study or as part of a class. It
will help you maximize your education in doing your
part to create a lifelong love affair with the man you
love.

This workbook is meant to help you understand and think more deeply about yourself, and to help you accept and inspire masculinity in the men you know, especially that special someone. If you are not married, it will help you know what to look for in a good man and how to maximize your chances to win his heart. It will help to teach you more about your own limitless worth and the important part you play in being a gate-keeper of civilization.

This is your personal and private workbook for your own use and growth. You should not be *required* to turn it in or share it with anyone. So please be as honest as you can.

Let's get started!

How do you rate your marriage?

Are you enjoying flowers…   …or weeds?

☐ **Extremely Happy**: My marriage is what I dreamed it would be. My husband cherishes me and would do anything in his power to make me happy. He is protective and devoted to me. He tells me he loves me regularly and we treasure spending time together.

☐ **Very Happy**: My husband loves me and we have a basically good relationship. We do have a few problems in our marriage, but I am dealing with it. He treats me with kindness most of the time, respects me and is thoughtful. He tells me he loves me occasionally.

☐ **Happy**: I have a marriage which I feel will endure. We have problems between us, and friction from time to time, but I believe he essentially loves me. He rarely expresses it though. I feel there is a bond between us despite any problems.

☐ **Mediocre**: Although we have no serious threatening problems, our marriage isn't what I once hoped. My husband is critical of me, negligent, and takes me for granted. I am critical of him too and he has a lot of habits that annoy me. He doesn't do spontaneous kind things for me or take me out on dates. He shows little interest in making our marriage better. He rarely tells me he appreciates or loves me.

☐ **Unhappy:** I am disappointed and unhappy with my marriage. My husband doesn't understand me and is critical and unkind. He spends most of his spare time away from home. He is usually cold and indifferent. He keeps his thoughts to himself, never tells me he loves me anymore and doesn't do anything for me that he doesn't feel pressure or obligation to do.

☐ **Very Unhappy:** My husband is cold and indifferent towards me and acts like he doesn't like or even respect me. He is often cruel and critical. He never does thoughtful things for me and doesn't appear to care about our home life or the children. I suspect he doesn't love me anymore.

☐ **Desperately Unhappy:** My husband has told me he doesn't love me anymore and that he doesn't enjoy being around me or perhaps even the children. He doesn't have an interest in our marriage or making any improvements and acts like marriage is some thing to be endured. He is sometimes physically, emotionally, verbally, or even sexually abusive. We have talked about divorce and I have wondered if he has had an affair (or he has told me he's having one). I have caught him lying to me.

Please check the rating that most closely applies to you. If parts do not apply, cross them out. Add what is necessary. Answer honestly please. You will have the best progress with an honest evaluation.

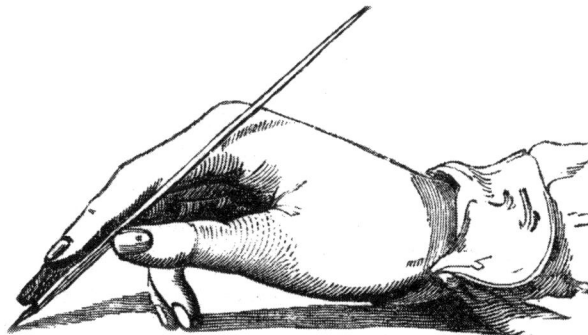

Describe the kind of marriage you want:

What counts in making a happy marriage
is not so much how compatible you are
but how you deal with incompatibility.

~Leo Tolstoy

For Singles:

How do you rate your romantic relationship/dating life?

Are you enjoying flowers...   ...or weeds?

☐ **Extremely Happy.** If you are in steady dating relationship, it's going very well. In fact, you are engaged or feel sure you will be soon. If you are dating but not exclusive, you have as many dates as you are comfortable with and go out with men who respect you and who you feel you can at least be friends with.

☐ **Very Happy.** If you are in a dating relationship, it's stable and seems to be moving forward. If you are not in exclusively dating, you have dates with various men you like and who like you. You date quite regularly and most of the dates are with men you like.

☐ **Happy.** You are either dating a man you are very attracted to and think you might grow to love, or you have a somewhat active and enjoyable dating life.

☐ **Mediocre.** If you are dating exclusively, you aren't sure of your feelings or are considering ending your relationship because you are having second thoughts. If you are not exclusive, you either don't date often, or are only asked out by men you aren't attracted to.

☐ Unhappy. If you are dating, you either are with a man who doesn't treat you the way he should, or you are finding you don't love him and are planning to end it. If you are not exclusive, you don't date often, feel there are few men to choose from, or are asked out by men you don't like or aren't attracted to.

☐ Very Unhappy. If you have been dating exclusively, you fight often or feel you are treated with disrespect, experiencing neglect or emotional and verbal abuse. If you are not dating exclusively, you date rarely and when you do, you aren't asked out by men you like or even find attractive. It is beginning to affect your feelings of worth.

☐ Desperately Unhappy. If you are in an exclusive relationship, you feel abused verbally, emotionally, physically, even sexually. If you are not in a relationship, you don't date and wonder what is wrong. It has affected your self-esteem.

Please check the rating that most closely applies to you. If parts do not apply, cross them out. Add what is necessary. Answer honestly please. You will have the best progress with an honest evaluation.

7

Describe the type of dating life or husband you would like to have:

Love thy neighbour—and if he happens to be tall, debonair and devastating, it will be that much easier.
~Mae West

Section 1
Reclaiming Femininity

Lesson 1

Chapter 1: The Deepest Kind of Love

Chapter 2: Your Limitless Worth

Chapter 1
The Deepest Kind of Love

1. What do you believe is the difference between infatuation and lasting romantic love?

To achieve a lifelong love-affair, you must believe in it and want it deeply. You must also work towards it as a goal, perfecting principles like charm, character, acceptance, and admiration; but also understand that mistakes will be made along the way and things won't always be perfect. In many ways, the perfection we seek is more about our intended destinations than our various states along the journey. But as the Timeless principles become part of your nature and you find yourself living them more fully, you will see amazing results that will transform your life and your relationships in the best ways.

2. How would you describe the difference between love and lust?

3. What do you want from your romantic relationship? Be as specific as you can.

Love is a condition in which the happiness of another person

is essential to your own.

~Robert Heinlein

Chapter 2
Your Limitless Worth

"If women didn't exist, all the money in the world would have no meaning."
~ Aristotle Onassis

4. What are some of your personal strengths? Write as many as you can, and don't feel bad if you struggle. You may not be accustomed to this sort of exercise, and you may have to think of some answers later, but you will be very glad you did this.

* Physical Attributes:

* Character Qualities:

* Virtues or skills as a woman, a wife, or as a girlfriend:

* Virtues as a mother or in any maternal or nurturing role such as a teacher, caregiver, mentor, etc.:

* Feminine Qualities:

*   Homemaking Skills:

*   Achievements:

*   Other:

Women are the
Gatekeepers of Civilization

Building and maintaining a strong and positive self-regard is essential to finding and nurturing a lifelong love-affair. We sometimes let the world and its environments get us down, which can cause us to forget our individual worth, or the value of women in general. To become a Fascinating Woman, we first begin with ourselves and this foundational sense of worth.

5. Describe femininity and how you can recognize it in your self or in another woman.

6. In what ways do you feel you express femininity well?

7. What does it mean to be a
   "Gatekeeper of Civilization?"

8. What does the word "mother" mean to you and what sorts of tasks does it involve?

9. What does it mean when we say that men are the "protectors, builders, and organizers of civilization?"

10. Why do men *need* women?

11. Who are some of the more inspiring women you know of, and why do they inspire you?

The contributions we add to the world can't be calculated.
Children need us, society needs us, men need us.
You are of great and limitless worth. Never underestimate
your value as a feminine woman!

Lesson 2

Chapter 3: Feminine Power

Chapter 4: Your Weakness Is A Strength

Chapter 3
Feminine Power

*Feminine power is the ability or skill to make the world **want** to change, rather than the masculine approach to persuade or force it to change. It is expressed best through influence while keeping our femininity intact. Our perspective is nurturing, empathetic, supportive and bonding. We are more open to reaching out and talking, even getting help with what we are trying to do. Instead of crashing through doors, we encourage doors to be opened for us.*

12. Describe masculine power.

13. Describe feminine power.

14. Can women employ masculine power? How?

15. What are some of the negative side effects for women who practice masculine power?

16. Why do the genders find it difficult to fully emulate each other's native power type?

17. In what ways can you be an exceptional woman even if you're never famous or wealthy?

18. Recall an event in which you employed feminine power or witnessed someone else using it effectively. Is it possible to abuse you feminine power? How?

Practice *at least one* of your feminine power base characteristics this week and write the results below. Consider your native senses of:

* Spirituality

* Delicacy

* Capacity to love

* Sensitivity

* Dignity

* Graciousness

* Gentleness

* Quiet strength

* Ability to understand men

* Charm

19. Describe the reactions of others when you have exercised feminine power. How did you feel?

20. Why does feminine influence tend to be longer lasting than overt masculine power?

As you practice and learn these skills, you will more fully understand the true influence you have. The remainder of this section will help you recognize, develop, and practice your unique influence and feminine power.

The Feminine Power of Martha Washington

$\mathcal{P}$ractically everyone has heard of George Washington—the first American president and general of the Continental Army during the Revolutionary War. Most have probably also heard of his wife, Martha, though not nearly as many understand the important heroic role she played in that conflict.

Martha was completely dedicated to her husband. Several times during the war she left her comfortable home at Mount Vernon to be with him during harsh winter months. Her goal was to cheer up George, who faced nearly insurmountable odds and discouragement with an ill-equipped and starving Army, as well as threats from his superiors to replace him as general.

Her presence in camp brought cheer to the soldiers and comfort to George. Martha never complained when required to live in extremely cramped quarters and her general good mood was infectious to all.

She began to work feverishly to improve morale, creating an atmosphere as close to Mount Vernon as she possibly could. The relaxed environment she inspired created a haven for her husband to retreat to at stressful times. Martha encouraged other generals to invite their wives to join her there and the ladies not only put on dinner parties and dances, but worked tirelessly in sewing circles, repairing tattered uniforms and in manufacturing new shirts and stockings. All these things dramatically improved the spirits of the troops.

Many of the women regarded Martha as a celebrity and were astonished to learn that instead of wearing fine clothing at the camp that befitted her social and financial situation, she wore plain and ordinary dresses that fit the austerity the colonies were forced to endure during the war.

It was clear that George and Martha adored each other. Nathaniel Greene wrote, "Mrs. Washington is excessively fond of the general and he of her; they are happy in each other."

While at Valley Forge, life was so dismal and George so discouraged that Martha joined him during that cold, difficult winter. They spent an hour every morning at breakfast together, alone. George felt safe to complain to Martha about all his woes. He used her as a sounding board for all the ideas he had to win the war. In that one room where no one could interrupt them, she could listen to him, support him, and help him process his feelings and plans.

We can all be our own version of Martha Washington. When we practice the timeless principles in Fascinating Womanhood and learn the art of understanding men and developing our own femininity, we have the best chance of not only having a lifelong romantic marriage, but truly becoming much more as a couple than we could alone. Your children, grandchildren, and beyond will remember you with love and honor for your contributions.

Chapter 4
Your Weakness is a Strength

In this cold and difficult world, women sometimes find themselves
at a physical disadvantage with men and can often feel vulnerable
as a consequence. And in the midst of such harsh realities, we can
sometimes forget our limitless value and compensating strengths –
that in fact it is we who are many times the stronger ones.

21. In what situations do you feel vulnerable?

22. How can your feminine vulnerabilities become strengths and therefore an *advantage?*

23. What is feminine courage?

24. Name an example of feminine courage that you have witnessed, or something courageous that you have accomplished yourself.

25. Describe the feminine perspective and what distinguishes it from the masculine.

26. Describe your personal needs for fulfillment and happiness.

"Women are never stronger than when they arm themselves

with their weakness."

~Marie de Vichy-Chamrond,
Marquise du Deffand, Letters to Voltaire

Lesson 3

Chapter 5: Femininity

Chapter 6: Feminine Appearance

27. What meaning comes to mind when you hear the word
"femininity"? Is it positive? Does the way
you define it personally differ from how
your friends (or society today) defines it?
Explain.

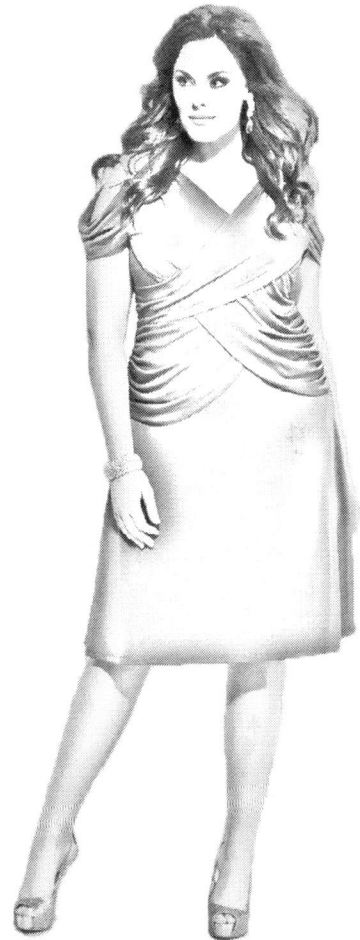

A woman who embraces her femininity
is a woman who knows her power.
~Kelly McNelig

28. Has some of your femininity been compromised due to the way you were raised? If so, how? If not, how did you escape feminist indoctrination?

29. Why, do you suppose, has femininity been mis-labeled as "weak"?

I'm very definitely a woman and I enjoy it.
~Marilyn Monroe

30. Do you see Fascinating Womanhood principles as a contrast to what you thought femininity was? If so, how?

31. In what ways have you found that emphasizing the differences between you and your man helps the most in your relationship?

"Women are always beautiful."

~Ville Valo
Finnish singer, songwriter and musician

Chapter 6
Feminine Appearance

Femininity is your greatest power. Embrace it!
~Stacey Martino

32. Why and when does appearance matter?

33. How do you feel when you make
an effort with your appearance?

34. What is your clothing style? Dramatic? Sporty? Classic? Romantic? Something uniquely your own?

35. What is androgyny? How does it affect femininity?

36. Have you noticed a difference in others' reactions to you when you look and act feminine, compared to an unfeminine appearance and manner?

37. What are the differences between being seductive and being feminine?

38. How can character affect appearance?

39. Have you known anyone whose character is reflected in their appearance? How can you tell?

40. What are pizza clothes? How do you feel when wearing clothes like this? If you don't wear pizza clothes, write how you *would* feel.

*Note: Pizza clothes are **not** necessary for messy or arduous tasks, such as painting, yard work, or even mud football. If you have a choice of what to wear or buy, always choose the prettier color, the better fit. Mend damaged areas and launder stains. If your clothes are too big, alter them or get rid of them. And if, for some crazy reason, you must wear pizza clothes, make sure your hair looks feminine and/or your makeup looks great. Cute, feminine shoes and jewelry always help too. As my husband Bob says, "Don't wear bald tires with your Mercedes!"*

Pizza Clothes
Multiple Choice Test

Circle the correct answer:

1. When you're sick, should you still consider your appearance?

a. No. Being sick is the perfect excuse to ignore how you look.

b. Yes. You should wear your finest evening gown with stiletto heels for your man.

c. Yes. Take a bath and wear pretty pyjamas. Brush your hair. It will perk up your spirits.

d. Yes. But everyone will understand if you wear pizza clothes and don't bathe.

2. What are pizza clothes good for?

a. Painting the house

b. Going to the gym

c. Helping your man fix the septic tank

d. Pizza clothes have no place in your closet. You're a lady.

Pizza Clothes

3. Scenario: You must wear jeans and a black t-shirt as your uniform at work. How can you make this ensemble more feminine and attractive?

a. A messy bun, minimal makeup, and heavy shoes

b. A feminine hairstyle, jewelry, light perfume, and/or carefully applied makeup

c. A feather boa or something similarly glamourous

d. Give up. There's no way to make that ensemble attractive.

4. What constitutes pizza clothes?

a. Clothes that are dirty, full of holes, have buttons missing, stained, in bad repair, etc.

b. Clothes that are stretched out, ill-fitting, frumpy, baggy or clearly out of fashion

c. Clothes that get you mistaken for a man constantly. "Excuse me, Sir… OH! I'm sorry!"

d. All the above

5. What do most men think of pizza clothes on their girl?

a. They can see the real you in their imaginations, so pizza clothes don't deter them.

b. As long as you have an amazing body underneath and a good personality, they're happy.

c. Most men just won't notice you in pizza clothes because you become invisible to them.

d. They wish you'd wear them more often so other men will stop ogling you.

NOT Pizza Clothes

40

41. What types of men might you attract if you choose to dress seductively in public?

42. How do you feel when/if you are dressed provocatively? What kind of reaction from men do you get?

43. How do you feel when you are dressed feminine*? What kind of reaction do you get?

*Contrary to popular belief, seductive clothing is not feminine. It lacks the class and dignity of femininity.

44. Why do women sometimes reject feminine appearance?

45. What are some ways you could pamper yourself more to appreciate your own unique femininity?

Embracing femininity for me means being gentle, kind and loving, being supportive, nurturing, happy. Radiating inner beauty through all that I am to those I love and meet...I love being a woman."

~Abigail, Australian model

Your Feminine Health

What are some ways that you can improve your health? Check any that apply and explain.

□ **Exercise:**

□ **Nutrition:**

□ **Sleep:**

□ **Weight Management:**

□ **Attitude/Stress Management:**

□ **Better posture:**

□ **Additional Self-Care:**

Lesson 4

Chapter 7: Charm

Chapter 7
Charm

Charm is more valuable than beauty.

You can resist beauty, but you can't resist charm.

~ Audrey Tautou

46. Why does everyone love being around a charming person? How do they make others feel?

47. Have you ever known a charming person? How did you feel when you were around them?

48. Without charm, why is *looking* feminine not enough?

49. How does charm empower a person?

50. With what aspects of charm have you made the most progress?

51. What facet(s) of charm would you like to work on?

52. Why does punctuality matter in your relationships with people?

53. Describe discipline and why it matters.

54. Describe the balance between wants, needs, and duty. Are your values basically intact?

55. What does it mean to love with your whole heart?

56. Why do manners matter?

57. Name some of the elements of being a successful conversationalist:

58. What are some subjects to avoid unless you know the person very well and know you are of a like mind?

59. Why can it be a problem when we are *too* "able"?

Practice the art of conversation this week with at least one person. If you're married, your husband is a great starting point. If you're not married, practice on either a boyfriend, a male family member, friend, or someone you'd like to get to know better. Briefly write what happened and then answer the questions below.

- How much listening did you do, as opposed to talking?

- Did you validate his thoughts or feelings? How?

- What was the result of your conversation practice?

- How did you feel when you focused on what he was saying?

Lesson 5

Chapter 8: Thanks for the Pants

1st Wave Feminism

60. What were some of the causes focused on in First-Wave Feminism? What were some of the aims?

WOMAN SUFFRAGE

61. In what ways do you feel the effects of First-Wave Feminism today?

62. What were some of the main goals of 2nd wave feminism?

63. How do you feel about 2nd wave feminism?

How has it impacted you?

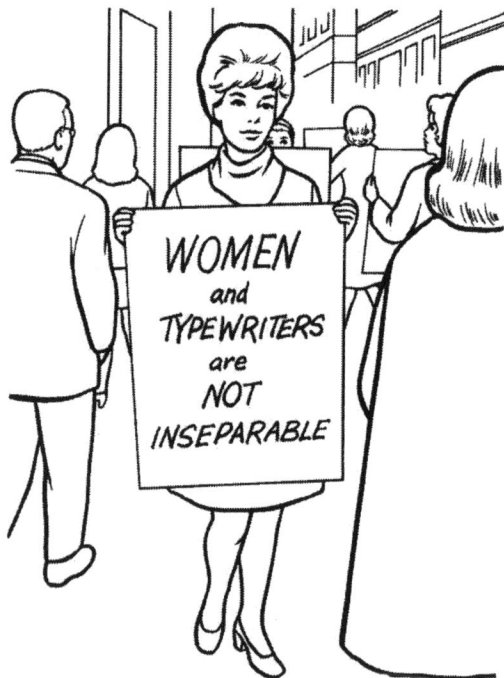

64. What are some of the goals of 3rd wave feminism?

65. What have you observed concerning modern-day feminism? What do you think its goals and values are?

66. Why do you think some women are perpetually angry with men?

WE WANT EVERYTHING

67. How has anger towards men fueled feminism?

68. In what ways have you seen women imitate or emulate men — or masculine qualities? What has been the result?

Always be a first-rate version of yourself,

instead of a second-rate version of somebody else.

~Judy Garland

69. What do you feel is expected of women in the modern era?

70. What are some of the positive accomplishments of feminism throughout modern history?

71. Name some ways we are marginalized by feminism.

72. How can feminism make women weak?

73. Can you think of an example in your life of a woman who has affected change in a feminine way? How did she do it? If you don't know anyone like this, what is a way someone could affect change without resorting to imitating masculine behavior?

Lesson 6

Chapter 9: Brain Matters

74. What are the three primary areas of your mind?

_____   _____   _____

75. In what direction do men's brains generally tend to be connected more strongly? What intellectual and emotional strengths does this connection give them?

76. What strengths do women have as a result of their brains tending to be more strongly connected from side to side? What drawbacks are there?

77. Do you consider yourself to be dominant in one part of your mind over others? Explain.

78. How can understanding your mind better help you in relationships?

79. How can understanding *his* mind better help in your relationship with him?

80. Have you ever thought "I'm my own worst enemy" or "My mind is playing tricks on me? Explain.

Your Survival Mind/Guard Dog

81. What is the purpose of your guard dog?

WE'RE HUNGRY!

82. How "domesticated" is your guard dog? Describe.

83. What kinds of things often cause your personal guard dog to bark or alert you?

84. What are some things that help to calm your guard dog?

ARFFF!
WOOF WOOF!

85. How does your guard dog help you?

86. What sorts of emotions signal to you that you are in a downstairs frame of mind?

87. How do you tend to behave towards people when you're in your downstairs mind? Would you say your behavior is generally constructive? If not, how could you improve this?

Does this room feel familiar? Which things are part of *your* normal "basement" or "downstairs" brain? What other things do you often see or hear in this place?

91. Why does it hurt you to stay too long in your downstairs?

A Proclamation on Downstairs Thinking

The other day I drove past a large store with a huge display of t-shirts for sale. One shirt that caught my attention boldly stated, "Nice Story Baby, Now Go Fix Me a Sandwich!" Do you wonder who that statement was aimed at? How does it make you feel? Marginalized? Used? The man who might buy and actually wear this t-shirt likely spends a lot of time in the downstairs, focused on himself, and has minimal respect for women. A red flag is proudly waving here.

Your Rational and Intuitive Minds

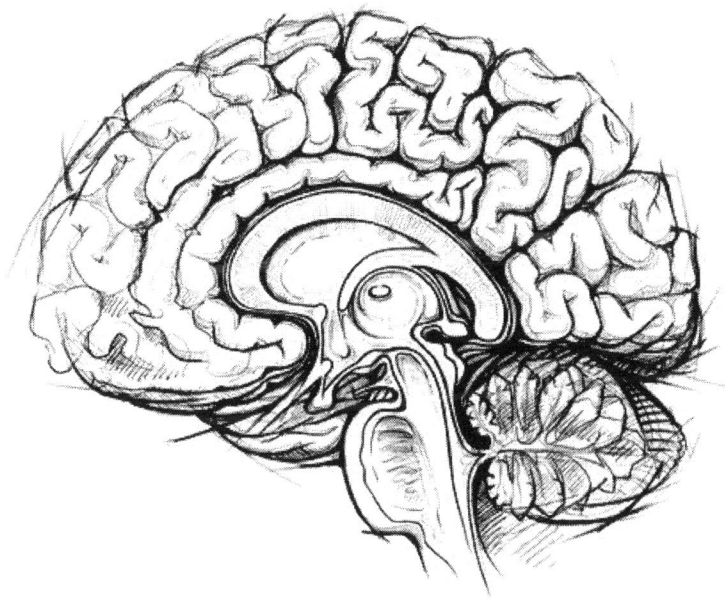

Knit a Circus Tent

The opposite of an "ah-ha" moment is when an idea your intuitive mind comes up is met with a huge "NO" from your rational mind. Years ago, on the back of a cereal box, there were instructions on how to knit a circus tent. The manufacturers knew people often read the backs of these boxes while eating breakfast. I can only surmise they must have thought it would be interesting marketing to put partial instructions on how to knit the tent with more instructions the next month. I guess the idea was to get people to keep buying cereal, so they could read continuing instructions. I don't know if anyone took it seriously, but it was fun to read. If most avid knitters were to take the construction of a circus tent out of yarn seriously, what might happen in the rational and intuitive parts of their brain? First, the intuitive part might kick in and believe "I can just picture it! I love to knit! I'm good at it. This would be fun! All my friends would be amazed!" But then the rational mind would quickly jump into the fray and say something like "Are you crazy? This makes no sense! You can't do that. You'll be a laughing stock. It will not only cost a fortune but what will you do with it? It wouldn't be practical; it would weigh a ton after a heavy rain. It will take forever to complete. What a waste of time!" Learning how to use your rational and intuitive minds in concert and working together make an unbeatable team. You will always have to deal with and calm your guard dog though, and the temptation to stay too long downstairs.

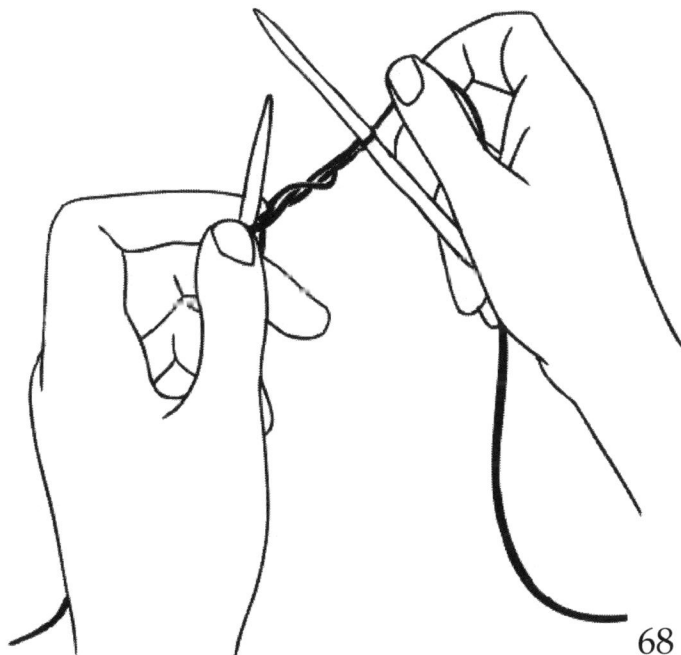

68

92. What are some ways you can think of that help to calm *his* guard dog?

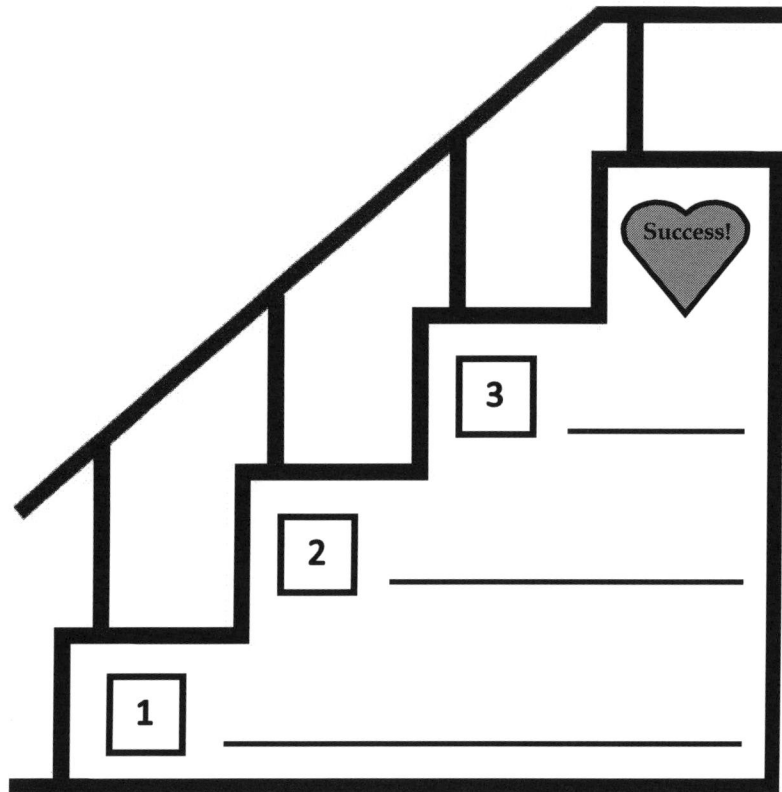

On the stairs, list 3 ideas of things that can help you get back to your upstairs mind:

Success!

3 _____

2 _____

1 _____

93. Describe what it feels like to go from a downstairs state of mind to an upstairs state.

*"The intuitive mind is a sacred gift;
the rational mind its servant.
We live in a culture that honors the servant
and has forgotten the gift."*
~ Albert Einstein

94. What is the motto of your rational mind? How does this govern your thoughts and actions?

95. What mental states signal to you that you are in a rational frame of mind?

96. What are your rational mind strengths and how do they benefit you?

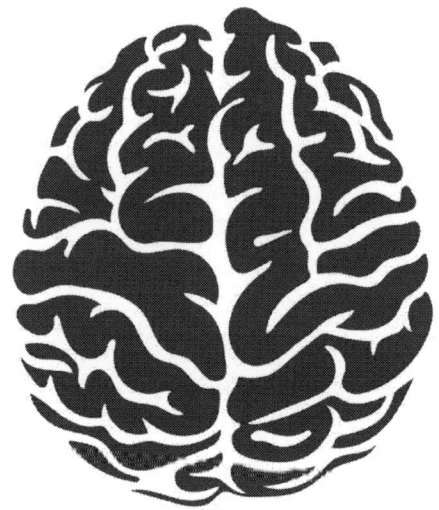

97. What impact does the rational mind have on your emotions?

98. What is the motto of your intuitive mind?

99. What are some of the main strengths of your intuitive mind?

100. What emotions signal to you that you are in an intuitive frame of mind?

101. How has your intuitive mind helped you? Provide an example.

102. What is the prolonged effect of an overactive intuitive mind?

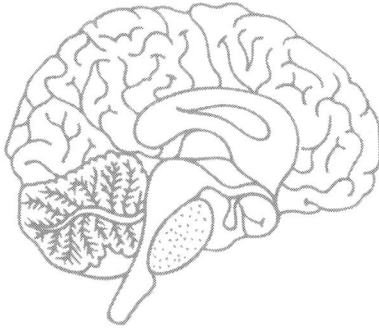

103. How are men's and women's brains different, and do the differences matter? Explain.

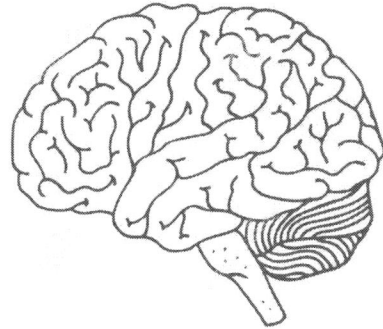

104. What kinds of things cause his guard dog to bark that might be different than yours? How can you help him calm his barking guard dog?

105. How does your approach to getting upstairs differ from his?

106. Describe an experience you have had where you felt like your entire brain was balanced.

Lesson 7

Chapter 10: Battling Your Inner Demons

Chapter 10
Battling Your Inner Demons

Gratitude: Your Secret Weapon

What are you grateful for? Below, list as many good things in your life as you can. The more distinct answers that you can write here, the more your answers will benefit you. Your ability to recall what you are grateful for is the most powerful tool you have in your battle with stress and your efforts to stay upstairs.

You may consider copying these answers in a separate place that you can refer to later.

107. Why are women more sensitive to negative emotion and vulnerability?

108. What have you worried about that never ended up happening?
                          Is there a pattern to your worries?
                          Explain.

109. Why are women more sensitive to negative emotion and vulnerability?

110. How has stress impacted your relationships?

111. How well do you manage the stress in your life?

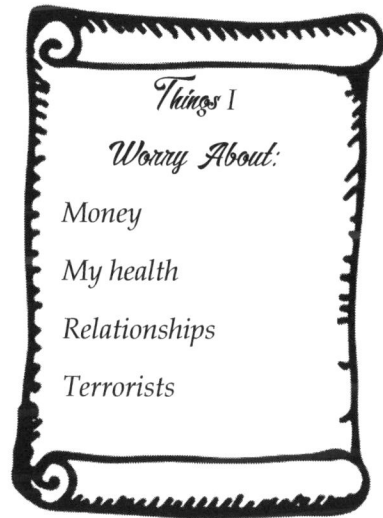

Things I

Worry About:

Money

My health

Relationships

Terrorists

112. How does each part of your brain try to help you manage stress?

113. What gets you upstairs the most effectively when you're over-whelmed?

114. Think of something bad that has happened to you. Can you think of something good that came from it?

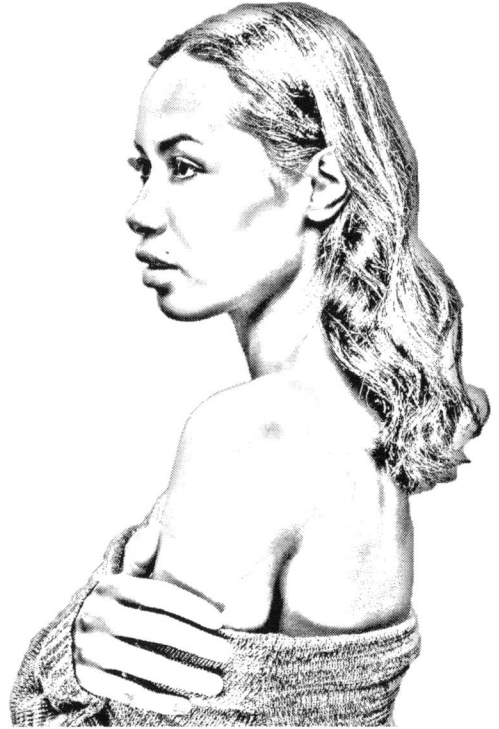

115. Describe and explain the "dopamine shower".

An ignorant state, stress is.
An emergency, it believes that everything is.

~ Yoda, Star Wars

Self Care Ideas

* Bathe regularly, with nice soaps or shampoos or bubble bath when possible

* Take care of your nails, your skin, and your hair

* Wink at yourself in the mirror when you brush your teeth

* Accept compliments graciously rather than deflect them

* Set boundaries with everyone you know

* Make your bed every day

* Dress as if you love yourself

* Take time for yourself when you can

* Be kind in your self-talk

* Forgive yourself for mistakes

* Follow your own personal code with integrity

* Keep promises you make to yourself and others

* Eat nutritious food, drink plenty of water

* Get lots of sleep when you can

* Smile when you say your own name to others

* Wear comfortable, attractive clothes that flatter you

* Congratulate yourself for daily small victories

* Walk away from toxic relationships

* Tell yourself that you're lovable and worthwhile

* Reward yourself in healthy ways, rather than gorging on guilty pleasures

* Replace negative mental chatter with positive and affirming thoughts

* Speak well of others—it will affect how you feel about yourself

* Learn how to say "No" when you need to; practice in the mirror if necessary

* Treat yourself with as much gentleness as you do those you love dearly

Section 1 Notes:

Section 2
Inspiring Masculinity

Chapter 11
Understanding Men

1. Why are men important?

2. What is the difference between noble masculinity and the sort of masculinity many describe as *toxic*?

Women are the real reason we get up every day. I am talking about real men. If there were no women, I would not even have to bathe. Because why would I care? ...I wake up for a woman every day of my life to make it happen for her.
~Steve Harvey

3. What do you look for in a truly masculine man?

4. In what ways do women tend to misunderstand men?

There are few things more frightening to a man than giving away his heart. And there are few things more comforting to a man than to know the woman he gave his heart to, will protect it with her life.
~Fawn Weaver

5. Why do women need to inspire masculinity?

6. Do you know—or have you known—a mature masculine man? How did he treat you? How did you feel around him? This could be a husband, father, uncle, brother, or any significant man in your life. It could also be someone from a book or movie. Please describe.

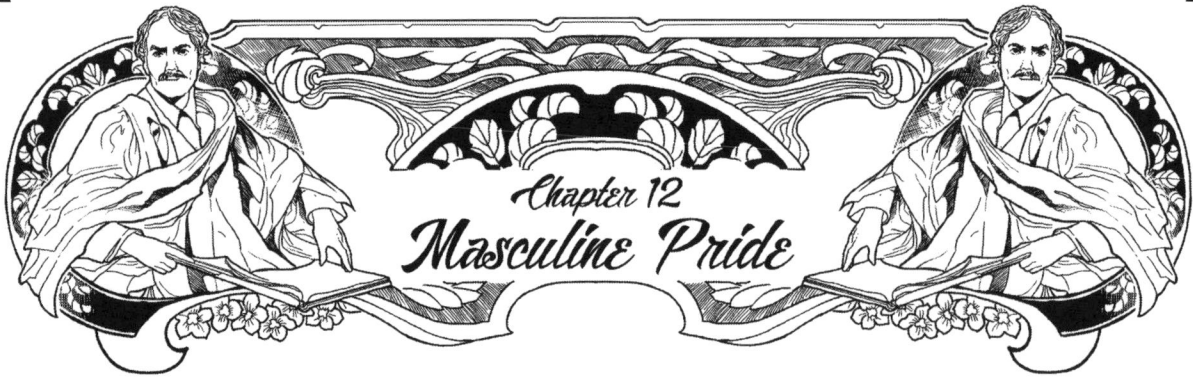

7. What wounds a man's pride and how can you avoid hurting him?

8. What are some areas of masculine vulnerability you can validate?

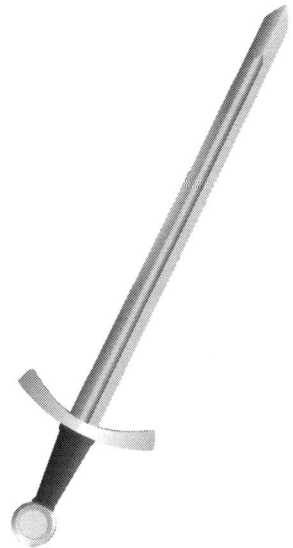

His Wall of Reserve

9. Describe a man's "wall of reserve."

10. How does a wall of reserve come down and what is your role in this process?

His Need to Protect and Provide

11. Why do masculine men feel a need to protect and provide for their loved ones?

12. Do you feel belittled by a man's need to protect and provide for you? If not, how do you feel about it?

Providing for the ones he loves and cares about, whether it's monetarily or with sweat equity, is part of a man's DNA, and if he loves and cares for you, this man will provide for you all these things with no limits.
~Steve Harvey

His Need to Be Your Hero

13. What attributes does your man have that make him a hero in your eyes?

14. In what areas does your man hold the potential for being more of a hero to you?

Men's Emotional Needs

15. What are some of a man's
emotional needs?

16. What needs of his are you good at validating?

17. In what ways could you improve validating his needs?

18. Have you ever wounded your man's pride, or any man's pride? Describe what you learned.

Lesson 9

Chapter 13
Making Him Number One

19. What does it mean to make your man number one?

20. Where do you and children fit into his being treated as number one?

21. How did you feel about him when you first fell in love? Describe.

22. How can you make him feel like he is number one?

Chapter 14
Acceptance

Being loved just as you are is the greatest currency on earth. It is immeasurable in value and can never truly be repaid.
~ Fawn Weaver

23. What does it mean to accept someone at face value?

24. Why is acceptance difficult?

25. Why do we try to change others?

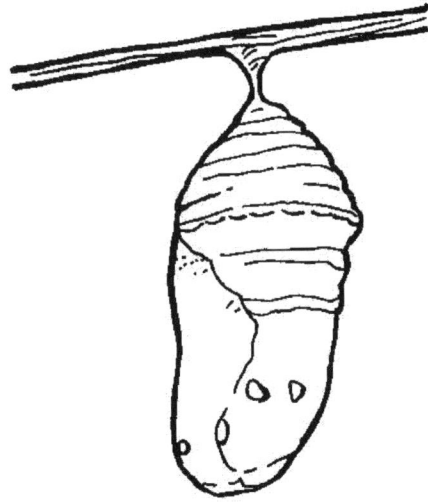

26. What tends to happen when we try to change someone?

A woman can't change a man because she loves him, a man
changes himself because he loves her.
~Anonymous

27. Has anyone ever tried to change you? How did it feel?

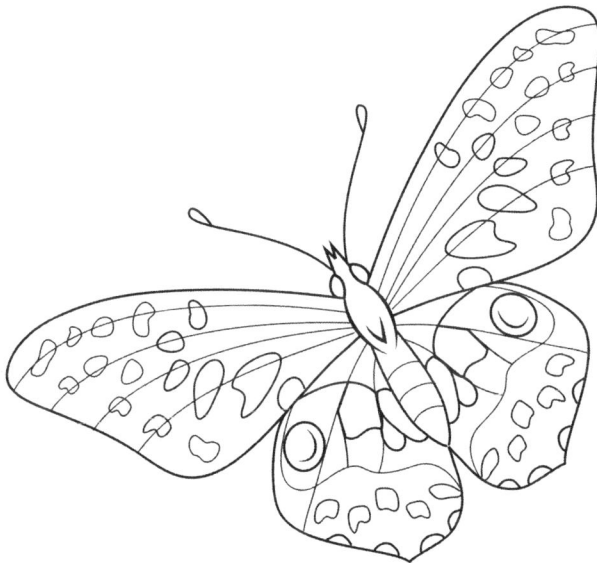

28. What is the impact of changing yourself?

*Success in marriage does not come merely through **finding** the right mate, but through **being** the right mate.*
~*Barnett Brickner*

Accepting a Man at Face Value

A Success Story

Before taking Fascinating Womanhood, I had practically given up on my marriage. In fact, two days before my first class, I had consulted a lawyer about getting a divorce from my "unbearable" husband. He drank too much, had no interest in us, and each weekend would take off to some extravagant city and spend his entire paycheck. When he learned I had seen an attorney, he begged me with tears in his eyes not to leave him. "I'll change, I'll do anything!" he pleaded. Finally, I was satisfied, for he had promised to change.

Then I had my first Fascinating Womanhood lesson on accepting him at face value. I had to admit that I make mistakes too. Could the fault be partly mine for not accepting him?

I went home and told him I accepted him the way he was. I said I had made a lot of mistakes in our marriage and would sincerely try to do better. A wonderful, though shocked expression appeared on his face and he said, "You mean, I can go spend all the money and you won't care?" "If you still want to after I'm fascinating, go ahead," I said with a smile. Things were better already.

He hasn't gone out one time since I've been practicing this philosophy! I still have a lot of work to do on all phases of it, but our marriage has become better each week, with each lesson. I only hope I can keep improving and may eventually earn his celestial love. Thank you for showing me the way.

Chapter 15
Admiration

29. Why do men prefer admiration over love?

30. What are some qualities you genuinely admire in your man?

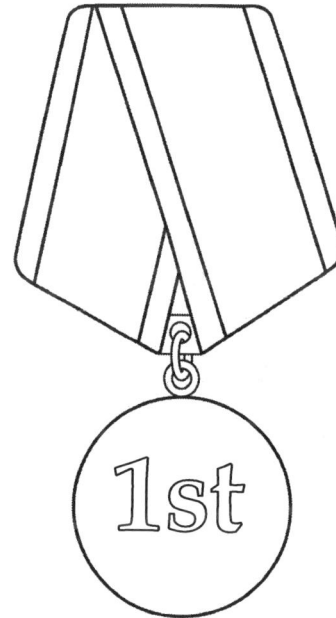

These are the things of which men think, who live: of their own selves and the dwelling place of their fathers; of their neighbors; of work and service; of rule and reason and women and children; of Beauty and Death and War.
~W.E.B. Du Bois

31. How can you expand your
admiration for him?

32. What are some areas in which almost all men crave admiration?

Sympathetic Understanding

33. Briefly describe sympathetic understanding.

34. What are some ways you can show sympathetic understanding to your man?

What men want and need:

Admiration

Physical Intimacy

To feel competent

A companion to dream of the future with

To be a hero

Words of praise

A home that's a refuge from daily cares

For his woman to be his biggest fan

Acceptance despite his flaws

A wife he's proud to show off to friends
and family

A life partner who is a trusted confidante

Someone to have fun with, laugh with

Someone to share sorrow and disappointment with

    —a support system

To pass on his thoughts, traditions, discoveries and dreams

Offspring—a continuation of his DNA

To build a family legacy

Comfort and companionship in old age

*Note: Can you think of anything your man wants or needs that you did not
see on this list? Write it here:*

35. What is a man's Pandora's Box?

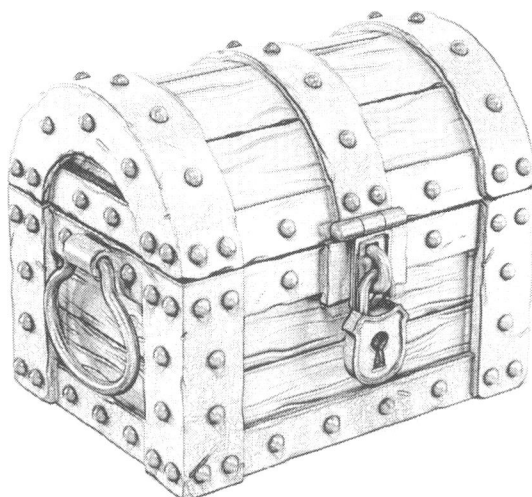

36. What is a Pandora's Box reaction like?

37. Why might he have kept his feelings to himself?

38. What wonderful things can happen when his Pandora's Box is emptied?

Note: You won't see a Pandora's box reaction if he hasn't built up
any resentments or wounds over some significant time.
Some women might feel they themselves need a Pandora's Box reaction,
but it is not usual for us. We tend to be much more verbal and
process our emotions more frequently by talking about them,
so ours don't tend to build up to such a critical level.

What a Pandora's Box Reaction is NOT:

A temper tantrum

A cover for a recurring anger problem

And excuse for emotional, physical or sexual abuse

A constantly occurring outburst

An expression of immaturity

A reason to panic

A time to lecture your man

What it IS:

An outburst of powerful emotions, pent up over time, that can sometimes spill out all at once. It can occur during the beginning stages of newfound or renewed trust in you after a period of hurt and distrust. It tends to come out when your man is starting to feel safe sharing his emotions with you once again.

Note: Not all relationships will have Pandora's Box reactions. They tend to accompany situations of extreme hurt and distress over long periods of time, sometimes years, and are usually caused by the suppression of feelings. In many cases, men have buried these emotions from hurts caused before we have even met them. Men who have difficulty expressing themselves verbally are often the most vulnerable to this type of reaction.

Section 2 Notes:

Section 3
Creating a Lifelong Love Affair

Lesson 10

Chapter 16: 4 Levels of Relationships

Chapter 16
Four Levels of Relationships

1. What are the four levels of intimacy? Describe each briefly.

_____

_____

_____

_____

2. Why is it ideal to develop the four levels of intimacy in a particular order? What could go wrong if you don't?

3. Describe an intellectual relationship. Why is it important to continue this after marriage?

4. If you are married, how do you keep your intellectual relationship intact? If you aren't married but are dating, is the intellectual part of your relationship strong? Describe. If you are not in a relationship, how can you develop your intellect now in preparation for a relationship?

5. Describe emotional intimacy.

6. What is the difference between a thought and a feeling?

7. Who is most comfortable talking about and showing emotion in your marriage or relationship? You, or your husband/boyfriend? Explain.

8. Why do many men *seem* less emotional?

9. In what way is your man deeply emotional?

10. How does an emotional relationship pre-
pare you for a deeper commitment?

11. How would you define spirituality?

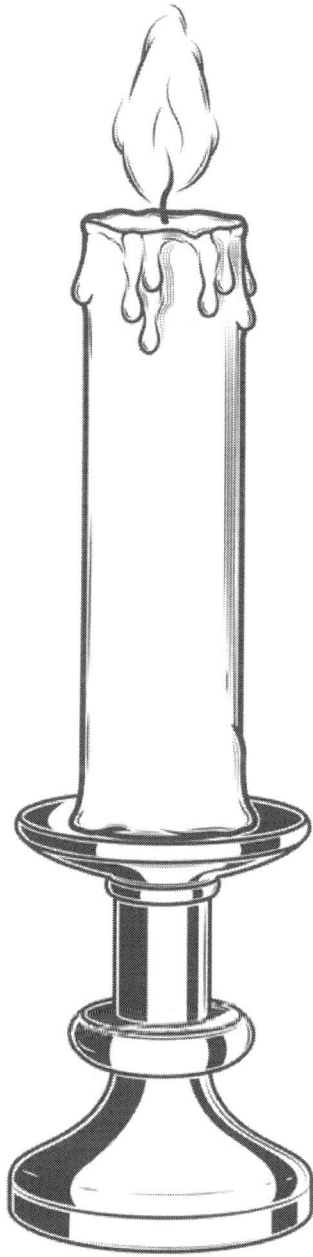

12. Is there difference between spirituality and being religious? Explain.

13. What is spiritual intimacy in the context of a relationship?

14. How does spirituality benefit people?

15. Under what circumstances do men feel comfortable sharing their spiritual intimacy?

16. Do you have a spiritual relationship with your husband/boyfriend? Describe. If you are single, what sort of spiritual relationship do you want with your future man?

17. What can you do to strengthen your spiritual relationship with your man?

18. What are some of the dangers of engaging in physical intimacy in a casual relationship?

19. Why is it emotionally high-risk for women to have sex before marriage?

20. Premarital sex is extremely common in modern society. What are some of the negative consequences you have seen as a result?

21. What areas of intimacy in your relationship could benefit from improvement?

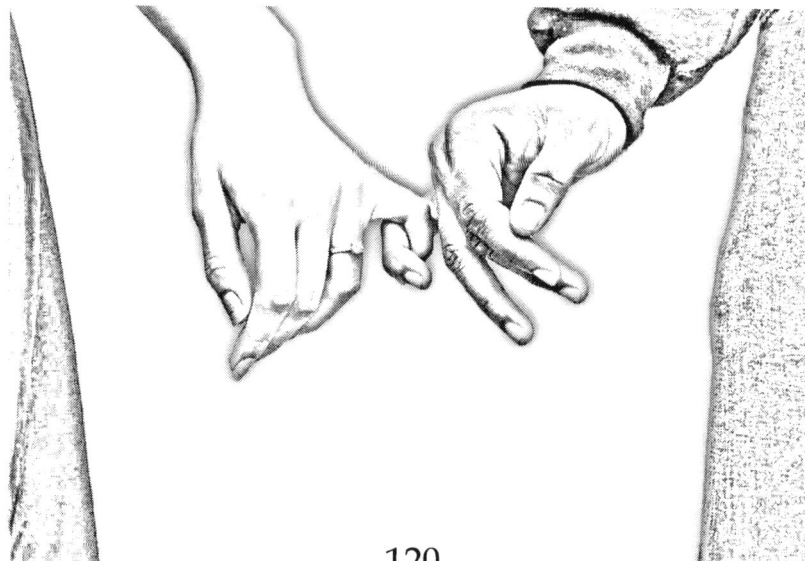

Lesson 11

Chapter 17: Masculine and Feminine Roles

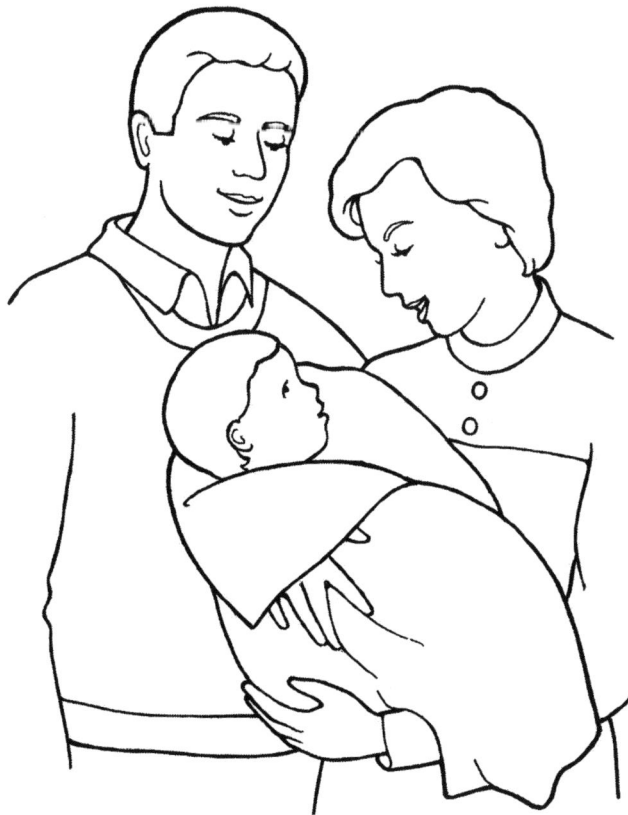

22. How does the experience of having a family benefit a person? A community? A nation?

23. If you are married with children, what were some of the reasons you wanted to start a family? If you are not married, do you want to start a family and why?

24. Do you identify more as a relationship leader or a task leader? How about your man? Explain.

25. What are the advantages of division of labor in the context of a family?

26. What is the role of a task leader?

27. What is the benefit of having a task leader in a family and what is the risk of having none?

28. What is the role of a relationship leader?

29. Can women make good task leaders? Explain.

30. Can men be good relationship leaders? Describe.

31. Why do men *tend* towards task leadership and women towards relationship leadership?

32. Can a task leader cover for a temporarily missing relationship leader? Can relationship leaders handle the task leader job for a period of time? Explain.

33. How can a task leader best support a relationship leader?

A strong marriage rarely has two strong people at the same time. It is a husband and wife who take turns being strong for each other in the moments when the other feels weak.
~Ashley Willis

The Importance of Fathers

Excerpts from a speech given by Barack Obama
to Apostolic Church of God in Chicago
in June 2008, prior to his election

Of all the rocks upon which we build our lives, we are reminded today that family is the most important. And we are called to recognize and honor how critical every father is to that foundation. They are teachers and coaches. They are mentors and role models. They are examples of success and the men who constantly push us toward it.

But if we are honest with ourselves, we'll admit that what too many fathers also are is missing — missing from too many lives and too many homes. They have abandoned their responsibilities, acting like boys instead of men. And the foundations of our families are weaker because of it.

We know the statistics — that children who grow up without a father are five times more likely to live in poverty and commit crime; nine times more likely to drop out of schools and 20 times more likely to end up in prison. They are more likely to have behavioral problems, or run away from home or become teenage parents themselves. And the foundations of our community are weaker because of it.

How many times in the last year has this city lost a child at the hands of another child? How many times have our hearts stopped in the middle of the night with the sound of a gunshot or a siren? How many How many times in the last year has this city lost a child at the hands of another child? How many times have our hearts stopped in the middle of the night with the

sound of a gunshot or a siren? How many teenagers have we seen hanging around on street corners when they should be sitting in a classroom? How many are sitting in prison when they should be working, or at least looking for a job? How many in this generation are we willing to lose to poverty or violence or addiction? How many?

Yes, we need more cops on the street. Yes, we need fewer guns in the hands of people who shouldn't have them. Yes, we need more money for our schools, and more outstanding teachers in the classroom, and more after-school programs for our children. Yes, we need more jobs and more job training and more opportunity in our communities.

But we also need families to raise our children. We need fathers to realize that responsibility does not end at conception. We need them to realize that what makes you a man is not the ability to have a child — it's the courage to raise one.

We need to help all the mothers out there who are raising these kids by themselves; the mothers who drop them off at school, go to work, pick up them up in the afternoon, work another shift, get dinner, make lunches, pay the bills, fix the house, and all the other things it takes both parents to do. So many of these women are doing a heroic job, but they need support. They need another parent. Their children need another parent. That's what keeps their foundation strong. It's what keeps the foundation of our country strong.

Excerpts from coverage by Politico Staff

34. Why do relationship leaders make good homemakers?

35. Why do task leaders tend to make good bread-winners?

Lesson 12

Chapter 18: Character

Chapter 19: Boundaries

Chapter 18
Character

Hard-working

36. Discuss your understanding of character.

37. How does character benefit a person and a relationship?

Honest

38. How does good character inspire the love of a good man?

Kind

39. What is the difference between happiness and pleasure?

40. What are some of your character strengths?

When women go wrong,
men go right after them.
~Mae West

41. What are some character traits you'd like to strengthen?

Loyal

42. How would you define courage? Do you consider yourself courageous? Explain.

43. What is humility and how does one recognize it in oneself and others?

44. What is your sense of honor and how do you recognize when someone has great honor?

Your priorities aren't what you say they are.
They are revealed by how you live.
~Marriage Today

48. How do you maintain a constant approach to self-improvement?

49. What are some benefits of learning to be a basically happy person?

50. How can character affect appearance?

"Whoever is careless with the truth in small matters cannot be trusted with important matters."
~ *Albert Einstein*

51. How would you describe "personal boundaries" to someone who had never heard the phrase before?

52. How can you determine what is safe and reasonable behavior for yourself and others?

53. How do boundaries benefit relation-ships?

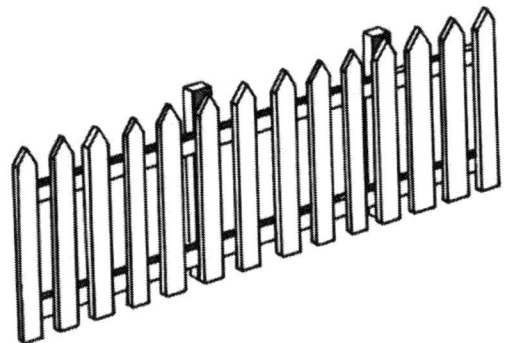

*You are not required to set yourself on fire
to keep other people warm.*
~Unknown

54. How does a lack of healthy boundaries hurt relationships?

55. What is the connection between healthy boundaries and honesty?

56. What can you do to improve the balance between your personal need for boundaries and your relationships with others?

Daring to set boundaries is about having the courage to love ourselves, even when we risk disappointing others.
~Brene Brown

57. Why do couples often find the ritual of relationship repair difficult?

58. How does relationship repair promote a lifelong love affair?

59. What might be a more effective way to express yourself when you feel the need to verbally process / vent?

Lesson 13

Chapter 20: Girlishness

Chapter 20
Girlishness

Childlikeness is an extreme girlishness. It is a quality of sauciness, spunk, innocence, trustfulness and tenderness all mixed into one. It is changefulness of emotion, from joyfulness to innocent anger. It is the charming qualities of a little girl.

~ Helen B. Andelin

60. What is the difference between influence and manipulation?

61. Describe girlishness in your own words.

62. Child*like*ness and child*ish*ness are very different. Can you explain how? Which one is similar to girlishness?

There is nothing more rare, nor more beautiful, than a woman being unapologetically herself; comfortable in her perfect imperfection.
To me, that is the essence of beauty.
~Steve Maraboli

Childish or Girlish?

Below is a list of common personality traits of children. Circle the traits that you think are good to emulate as an adult. Draw a star beside the ones you already possess. Some traits have pros and cons. You may want to think creatively with this exercise.

Speaking openly and plainly

Bossiness

Asking lots of questions

Being blunt

Showing curiosity

Asking for things directly

Being clingy

Hiding your mistakes

Possessiveness

Quick to forgive

Adaptability

Non-judgmental

Honest when angry

Temper tantrums

Animated when receiving gifts

Doesn't hold grudges

Not afraid to cry

Dramatic

An open book

Teachable

Enthusiastic

Volatile when sleepy

Tendency to exaggerate

Willingness to change

Anger dissipates quickly

Easy smiles and laughter

Trusting

Affectionate

Lack of ego, sarcasm

Messy when eating

Enjoys dancing

Uninhibited

Demonstrative

Playful

Nothing is worth more than laughter. It is strength to laugh and to abandon oneself, to be light.
~Frida Kahlo

63. How can girlishness diffuse tension or change a general mood?

64. When is practicing girlish displeasure inappropriate?

65. Why do men love girlishness in us?

Girlish Displeasure Quiz

One of the most misunderstood principles in Fascinating Womanhood is that of childlike anger, or "girlish displeasure". But it's so important because it can help diffuse tense situations with our men. Below is a fantastic example of a female movie character who is the master (or mistress) of the principle. In fact, this scene is a great blueprint for solving a lot of situations where your man has been careless or thoughtless.

This excerpt is from the classic film **Giant**, starring Elizabeth Taylor as Leslie, a well-bred and feminine girl who marries tough Texas rancher Jordan, played by Rock Hudson. In this scene, Leslie has just lost her temper at her husband and his friends, who excluded her from their evening "man talk" in a way she finds chauvinistic. She storms off to bed, and now her husband has finished downstairs and is joining her in the bedroom.

Please read, and then answer the questions that follow:

(Jordan comes in the room and takes his boots off one at a time, throwing them very loudly on the floor to wake up his wife.)

Leslie: I must have dropped off. Darling, I *am* sorry about my caveman speech. I'll apologize to the others first thing, I promise.

Jordan: That's big of you. (raising his voice) You certainly distinguished yourself this evening.

Leslie: Shh, they can hear.

Jordan: Hear? They heard you already. Every word you said out there. We "date back 100,000 years".

Leslie: I said I was sorry about the name-calling. It was very impolite, I know. But in principle, I was absolutely right.

Jordan: You come down here and try to tell us how to run things. Insulting my friends and everything. Now you look here, Leslie. You're my wife, Mrs. Jordan Benedict. I'm asking you, when will you settle down and behave like everybody else?

Leslie: Never!

Jordan: (yelling) Who do you think you are, anyhow? Joan of Arc, or something? (he heads toward the adjoining guest room)

Leslie: Jordan, where are you going? (softer voice) Jordan, take off your hat.

Jordan: (still yelling) Carrying on like Carrie Nation! Preaching stuff that's none of your business, fixing the world. Why don't you join a club?

Leslie: Honestly, Jordan. You make me sound just awful. I'm not all that bad. You knew what a frightful girl I was when you married me. I did not deceive you, sir. From the first moment, I couldn't have been more unpleasant. (softer voice again) Anyway, you're stuck with me. (smiles at him gently)

Jordan: Yes, I guess.

Leslie: Honey, take your hat off. (he takes it off, sullen and suddenly bashful). Besides...you love me very much.

Jordan: (softer voice) That fine mind of yours gets pretty repulsive at times.

Leslie: That's not what you told me on the train. (their honeymoon)

Jordan: (blushing) Now you're gonna throw that up to me. I thought what we... I thought what we said on the train was in confidence.

Leslie: (smiling to herself at his absurd comment) Of course, darling. But I'll never forget a single word you say to me. You can be pretty wonderful at times. (sexy voice) Come on, partner. Why don't you kick off your spurs?

(Scene cuts to morning, and it's clear they had a very romantic night)

146

Questions:

1. Do you think Leslie was justified in being offended at not being included in her husband's "man talk"? If so why?

2. Why do you think Jordan was so angry with Leslie, aside from the reasons he gave?

3. At what point did Leslie change her tactic and stop escalating the argument? What do you think went through her mind at that moment?

4. What did Leslie say or do to diffuse the situation? What was childlike or girlish about her reactions? How was she "saucy" or "spunky"?

5. Can you see why Jordan would melt when he did? Why his anger disappeared? Explain.

6. Sometimes our instinct kicks in before we have time to think. How would your normal instinct tell you to react to something like this?

7. If Leslie could have gone back in time, what could she have done differently in order to settle this problem between herself and Jordan?

66. Imagine a time when your man was cross with you. How might you have responded with girlish displeasure? Explain the context and your potential responses.

67. How can a woman feel or express fear and still be strong?

68. What is girlish appreciation and why does it make men feel good?

69. This week, practice girlish appreciation at least once and describe your experience:

70. Describe girlish trust.

71. How does girlish trust differ in marriage versus dating? (Also see Notes for Single Women)

72. In what ways do you need to trust your man?

73. What are some of the best
ways to ask for things in a
feminine way?

74. What tends to happen when we hint with men?

75. What tends to happen when we demand things?

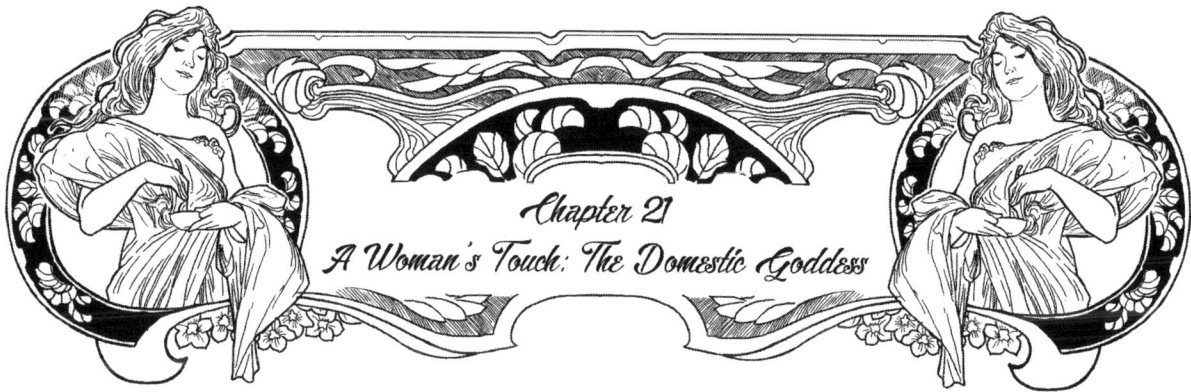

"Homemaking is surely in reality the most important work in the world. What do ships, railways, mines, cars, government etc. exist for except that people may be fed, warmed and safe in their own homes? The homemakers job is one for which all others exist"
~ C.S. Lewis

76. What role does home environment play in relationships?

Decorating is not about making stage sets, it's not about making pretty pictures for the magazines; it's really about creating a quality of life, a beauty that nourishes the soul.
~Albert Hadley

77. Describe an aspect of creating atmosphere at which you excel or which you enjoy.

78. What ways can you improve aroma in your home to create a better atmosphere?

I have always thought that there is no more fruitful source of family discontent than a housewife's badly cooked dinners and untidy ways.
~Isabella Barton

79. What are some things you can do to improve the visual atmosphere in your home?

80. How can you use pleasant sounds to create a warm environment in your home?

81. Why is taste, or good food, an important element of creating atmosphere?

82. What are your favorite food smells? What are *his* favorite?

83. Are there any dishes you wish you were more skilled at?

84. Do you like to cook? Do you have a specialty you love to make? Describe how you do it.

85. Can you think of at least one way you might improve the experience of touch in your home?

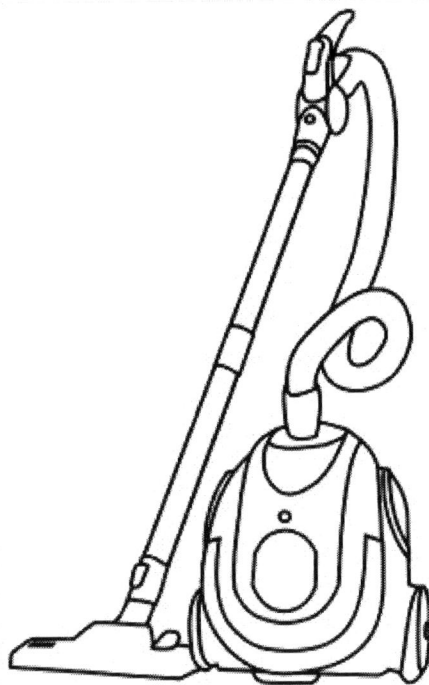

86. List any other homemaking skills you are good at or would love to learn such as crochet, gardening, etc.

Love is the thing that enables a woman to sing while she mops up the floor after her husband has walked across it in his barn boots.
~Hoosier Farmer

159

Possible Homemaking Skill
(Can you think of more?)

Giving massages

Keeping peace

Gardening

Creating a library

Home repair

Landscaping

Organizing

Decorating for holidays

Bottling food

Spiritual harmony

Party hostess

Sewing

Bringing laughter into a room

Caring for family photos

Cheerful attitude

Cooking

Food storage

Planning games & activities

Making people feel comfortable

Cleaning

Flower arranging

Playing beautiful music

Upholstery

Interior design

Creating a feeling of safety

First Aid

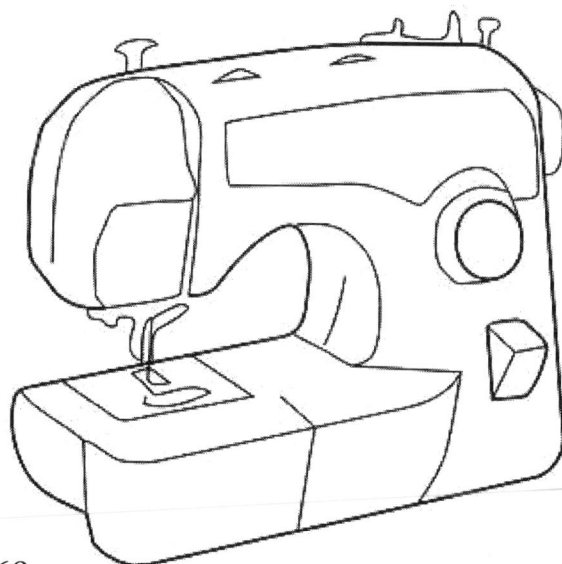

Creating Atmosphere:
Focus on the 5 Senses

Cooking aromas, clean smells, scented candles, flowers

Music, soft voice, crackling fire, clocks ticking

Slippers, nice fabrics, temperature, massage, soft carpet

Food variety: temperature, flavor, color, texture, culture

Nice lighting, pleasant design, colors, shapes, patterns

Home Sweet Home

What Kind of Man do you Want?

Are you looking for The One? Write down the qualities you would like in your ideal man, husband and father of your children.

Now list the qualities your ideal man will deserve and likely be looking for in his ideal woman, wife, and mother of his children.

Note: Focus on developing the skills and qualities you believe
he will be looking for, and you will have the best chance of
attracting the sort of man who closely resembles your ideal.
You don't have to be perfect and neither does he!

Read the following example of a woman who was able to im-prove herself, become more feminine, and find a man who cherishes her. Then answer the questions below:

I'll Never Marry Again

I must tell someone or I will burst, I am so very happy. I was divorced, very bitter and unhappy, forty years of age, the future dim, and a young child. I had attended Fascinating Womanhood classes. My sister asked if I would go out with a man. She kept at me, so I said I would go.

The first half of the evening, I had a chip on my shoulder, but he was so nice. Then a bell in my head rang—Fascinating Womanhood. He had been divorced nine years. Both of us said we never wanted to marry again. I practiced Fascinating Womanhood, but not to gain a husband. He said I had to be the most perfect woman on earth. We fell in love. We got married. He said that all women changed for the worse after they got married, but that I had changed for the better.

I live Fascinating Womanhood in every way. I have never seen a person so happy as my husband. He buys special little things and surprises me with "get dressed, I want to take you out and show you off." I am forty years old and cannot swim a stroke. He asked if I would swim to him. With little girl-like trust, I swam to him, not well, but I made it, sputtering. He said it was the proudest day of his life. He took me out and bought me two new bathing suits. It makes me happy when I see the complete joy on my husband's face when I do something extra for him.

Because of the book and classes, I was able to practice Fascinating Womanhood right from the start. God bless Fascinating Womanhood. It's made a man, a woman, and a child very happy.

1. What do you think is important about this woman working on herself "not to gain a husband"?

2. Can you guess what this woman changed about herself that delights her husband so much? Which Timeless principles might she have worked on?

Part A:

If you are dating frequently/already in a relationship:

Have you ever had an experience where a man said he wasn't ready for marriage? If so, please describe:

Does your man have a career or plan for a career? Explain.

What sorts of fun or romantic things do you like to do together?

Do you have deep conversations, and what have been some of your more meaningful ones?

What are his greatest priorities in life?

Are there any personal concerns that hold you or him back from progress in the relationship?

What is his relationship like with his family? What is yours like with his family?

What are his and your dispositions towards marriage in general?

How does he treat strangers in your presence?

I don't trust anyone who's nice to me but rude to the waiter. Because they would treat me the same way if I were in that position.
~Muhammad Ali

How is he with children? Do children like him?

Is he thoughtful with you? Explain.

How would you grade his
honesty?

What is his sense of humor like?

What are some things you appreciate about your boyfriend's manliness? Be specific.

What are some traits you can develop in yourself that will help inspire a proposal from him?

Part B:

If you are still looking for Mr. Right

Do you have any experience with online dating? How did (or do) you feel about it?

What types of men have you admired?

Are there certain types of men that you feel you often get "stuck" with? What have you disliked about them?

What areas of your life could you change that might fix this situation? *(Hint: you may want to review the chapters in Timeless about charm, boundaries, character and girlishness, or any other chapters that you feel might help you.)*

Have close friends or former dating partners ever suggested improvements you could make regarding your character, behavior, charm or appearance? Were any of these suggestions fair evaluations? How did you feel about it, and did you implement the suggestions?

What qualities do you already have that the man of your dreams will love (if he becomes aware of them)? How can you make the men around you more aware of these qualities?

Are there any types of male physical characteristics that you find unattractive? Describe.

Do you consider yourself very picky about dating partners? Are the things you are picky about vital to your future happiness in marriage? Explain your reasoning either way, whether you are too picky or not picky enough.

Which parts of your personality and behavior with men could use a little refining?

Have you ever had an experience where a man said he wasn't ready for marriage? If so, please describe:

What have you read in this book that can help you in your search for a life partner?

Good Ways to Get a Man's Attention

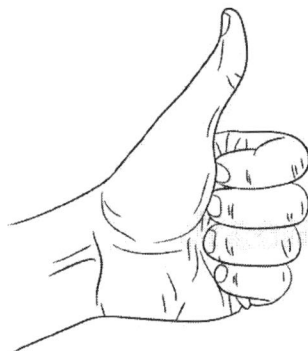

Dressing up ALWAYS — you never know where you'll meet him, even when you're out buying medicine while sick, or taking out the trash! First impressions are so important. Make sure to smell nice too, especially your hair. Just a fresh, clean scent. He'll be mesmerized when you walk by!

Not traveling in packs of females — men can find it extremely intimidating to approach your entire group of girl friends, no matter how pretty you are. And it's much easier for men to spot you when you're flying solo. This doesn't mean you shouldn't socialize. But try to move around the room and not stay in one conversation too long.

Wearing something unusual — make it easier for men to start a conversation (a strange brooch that he can't help but ask you about, a hair ornament that looks fun to play with, a fluffy sweater or scarf that makes him wonder how soft the fabric would feel if he dared touch it…).

Not hiding your talents — if you have a hobby or pastime that you enjoy, enter something you created into a contest or sign up for a talent show. If you have a special skill like dancing or cooking or languages, teach free classes in the community. Do you enjoy writing? Try getting something published in a magazine or local newspaper. Not only are these things great ways to network and meet new people, but they also help keep you "upstairs".

Not being too aware of your surroundings/too self-conscious — it's best to lose yourself in the moment and stop worrying about being noticed. Men tend to be fascinated by a woman who isn't looking.

Eye contact — yes, you shouldn't be constantly roving the room with your eyes. But when you do catch that handsome stranger's glance, try looking deeply into his eyes for 3 seconds...and then lower your eyes as if you're suddenly shy. Most men say this makes their hearts flutter wildly. It's a flirting secret as old as the hills, and men do it too!

Serving others and being busy — being a woman of kind and generous character, and a strong work ethic, is very attractive.

Being the one to say goodbye first — this is for conversations that are either in person or on the phone. It shows that you value your time and are not too clingy. Men want to know initially that you won't be hanging all over them constantly. They need space, especially early on.

Having a life and going places — make for yourself a fulfilling life he will want to be part of! You will be happier in the meantime anyway. And happiness is one of the most irresistible traits you could possess.

Asking and listening — practice the art of conversation on everyone you meet. Be sure to **ask** lots of open-ended questions, **listen** intently (without interrupting) to the answers, and then **remember** what you learned to enhance future conversations. Make this part of your personality, doing this with males and females alike. It will become second nature to you, and people (including men!) will constantly want to talk with you.

Stillness — not being fidgety or hyperactive; men are drawn to dignity and poise, and are often repelled by a woman with constant jitters.

Being feminine in the way you talk, move, and treat people — femininity is intoxicating to males, like a dreamy perfume. And it's in your blood!

Speaking kindly of others — men appreciate a soft-spoken woman who is generous in her opinion of others. It's an indication that she will be generous with him as well, which builds his confidence with you.

Being tactile — there is a fine art to showing affection with people you don't know well. A quick hug, a reassuring squeeze of the hand, or resting a hand on the shoulder while chatting, perhaps even resting your chin on their head if they're seated and you're standing. This should be practiced on both men and women, depending on your comfort level with them. Try it with family or close friends first if you're nervous. It will become a normal part of who you are. If someone says you're invading their bubble, back off, but most humans are starved for physical touch. It reassures them that they're wanted.

Touching his shoulder or forearm gently, and briefly — this one is directly related to the suggestion above, but is more specifically directed at the man you're interested in. It's also tried and true, and quite universal; a warm, non-threatening way to let a man know you are not just interested in who he is, but that you find him physically attractive.

Admiring him for his masculine traits — it's so easy, and it's FREE, to validate people. Make a practice of complimenting everyone you meet. Look for valuable qualities in others. This should be a part of you so that when you tell him how manly he is for something very specific, it will feel absolutely natural to do so.

Being socially generous — laugh at other people's jokes, build others up for their accomplishments, share their excitements rather than eclipse them, try to relate to their frustrations, defend the underdogs. Be **that** woman.

Bad Ways to Get a Man's Attention

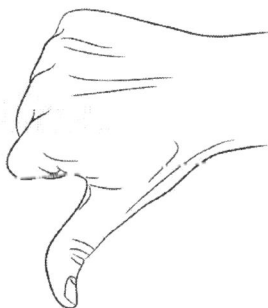

Competing with him — he'll tend to treat you more like a man, a "bro". Of course there's nothing wrong with having fun and trying to win when you play football or a board game together, but don't be vicious, and definitely don't be a sore loser (or worse, a bad winner).

Belittling him — some women think this is a good way to flirt; it's not. Being sassy and girlish is one thing, cutting him down is another — especially if you do it in front of his friends. And the damage you can do to a budding relationship can be permanent.

Complaining loudly about your life or surroundings — it's not charming and shows a lack of character. Nobody enjoys being around a complainer. Why should a charming man enjoy it?

Being too materialistic — if you make it known that you only date men who drive Mercedes or wear custom tailored suits, you not only rule out a lot of great men who are still seeking their fortune, but you let the men with money know that you're shallow. My husband Bob said he once went out with a girl who checked the neck of his shirt to make sure he was wearing a designer label. That relationship didn't last very long.

Gossiping about him — this damages his trust very quickly; he will not forget it. Men tend to be intensely private about personal things. And a lot of gossip isn't even true in the first place! Why would you spread that?

Being catty about others, hoping he'll find you "amusing" — men detest cattiness in females. Are you familiar with Pride and Prejudice? How far did the back-biting, critical Caroline Bingley go with her dream man, Mr. Darcy?   Exactly.

Poor hygiene — this should be fairly obvious. On the flip side, it helps so much when you smell very nice, whether it's the clean smell of having freshly showered, or a light and feminine perfume. Body odor and bad breath are huge turnoffs. So are greasy hair, dirt under fingernails, and soiled clothing. Even if you don't mind a smelly man with poor hygiene, you owe it to yourself and your friends (and **society**) to at least keep yourself looking and smelling presentable.

Dressing in a skimpy or seductive way — this shows a lack of self-esteem as well as a low class mentality. The right man will find you gorgeous without having a clear view of your cleavage or glimpsing a thong through a   transparent lace skirt. There's feminine, and then there's cheap. Choose   feminine, choose class. Men love class.

Chasing him around, staring at him, or stalking him — this makes you look desperate and turns men off. They want their boundaries respected, and they admire a woman with clear boundaries. Being aggressive invades his bubble, and it cheats him out of the fun of chasing YOU.

Not keeping your promises — a man needs to know that he can trust you with things that are both small and big. If you tell him you'll meet him at 5:30 pm, be there at 5:30 pm. If you promise not to flirt with other men, keep your word. Are you dreaming of a lifelong love affair where the romance never dies? That starts with promises you make to each other that are honoured and kept.

Being loud or obnoxious — either one is horribly unfeminine and tacky. And they're both common traits of insecure people. There are much better ways to get noticed.

Using coarse language or affecting manly speech — this greatly decreases your appeal, because it decreases the contrast between your femininity and his masculinity. If he wants filthy jokes, or someone saying "Check out my smelly feet!", he can hang out with his male friends. He's looking for something different with you. Something new and lovely.

Self-deprecation — he doesn't want to hear about your sweaty thighs, the bump on your nose, your bad singing voice, your poor grades in school or your lack of options in the dating world. Keep your chin up and love yourself. Pointing out your own flaws teaches people to notice them more, and makes prospective partners or friends worry that you'll be hard on them for THEIR flaws as well.

Lowering your standards — if you tell your man something is against your personal code, and then he sees you change your mind and do it anyway, he'll see that you don't stick to your standards. This is all about developing your character. Don't cheapen yourself for anyone.

Spilling his secrets — even worse than gossip, telling people things he's confided to you privately is one of the worst ways you can betray your man. It destroys his trust, and he will be less likely to share his feelings with you again. You can't build a lasting relationship where there's no trust.

Flirting with his friends — some girls think a sneaky way to get to a man is by becoming chummy with his buddies. This can backfire in so many ways. It's better to focus on the man you want so he doesn't get the wrong impression about you.

Note: Before you think about searching for Mr. Right, make sure you're working on your personal character, your attitude and femininity. It's crucial that you are sincere and honest in your behaviour. **These suggestions are not tricks to lure men into your trap**, *they are things that will come naturally when you focus on the needs of others, as well as working on yourself.*

The Rat Filter

How to Tell if He's a Keeper

Are there some qualities in a man that would be deal breakers for you if you were to become aware of them?

What are some traits you should watch out for?

Have you ever dated a man you suspected beforehand was a rat? How did it turn out? Were you right or wrong?

Name some places that are **not** ideal to meet eligible men.

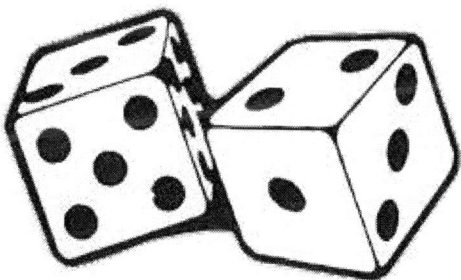

Note: It's not a good idea to meet people while under the influence of alcohol and drugs. Clubs and bars are sometimes considered prime places for singles to meet, but meeting men this way is actually high-risk behavior because honesty and true character in others is more difficult to judge when people are "under the influence". Yes, you can be in the fortunate minority if this works out for you, but do you really want to gamble with your future?

Places to Meet Men

(...that are NOT night clubs or bars)

Service projects, soup kitchens — where people CARE and serve freely

Churches or church group activities — even if you're not a member

Libraries — men who read or study are a great bet

Clubs where men play sports or games — so many ACTIVE men there

Jobs (finance, computers, science, hardware stores, airports, business, car lots) — if you work at these jobs, you'll know more men in general

Monster truck rallies and car races, rodeos — masculine places

Festivals (cultural, especially) — the crowd numbers are in your favor

Classes with a masculine edge — ex. take a class on kung fu or mechanics

University/college — not just in classes, you can meet men on campus

The gym — men who work out regularly care about their health and have constant endorphins pumping, so they tend to be happier

Online — make sure to use the rat filter and/or meet through friends

Campaign headquarters offices — find men who care about their world, and hopefully share your political views as well.

Stores and outdoor markets—places men love to shop or sell items (electronics, sporting goods, home repair, farmers markets)—be your friendly self and chat up other customers or store clerks. Network.

Police, firemen or military dinners/dances—there will be so many men there who work hard. Find friends who can get you invited.

Traveling—talk to men on airplanes, in foreign street markets, touring a shrine, riding horses or buses, (try to choose public places with other people around)

Through friends—one of the safest and best ways to meet men

Friends of friends—this is why networking is so important for you

Going OUT and talking to everyone—don't be a hermit

Coffee shops—men who seem glued to business on laptops or talking to friends (especially other men) are a nice bet if you can throw some gentle charm their way without disrupting their work!

Hospitals—volunteering there is a simple way to do this; hospitals are full of intelligent, hard-working men

Parties you throw at your home—believe it or not, this is part of networking because you never know which guest will bring a dreamy, available male friend, brother, uncle, son...

Notes:

Sullivan Ballou Love Letter

Sullivan Ballou was a Union soldier during the American Civil War. He is best known and remembered for this final letter he wrote to his wife during the same month he was killed at the Battle of Bull Run. This is a wonderful example of a couple that had built a strong and enduring romantic marriage — a lifelong love affair that, according to Sullivan, will endure beyond the grave.

July the 14th, 1861

Washington D.C.

My very dear Sarah,

The indications are very strong that we shall move in a few days — perhaps tomorrow. Lest I should not be able to write you again, I feel impelled to write lines that may fall under your eye when I shall be no more.

Our movement may be one of a few days duration and full of pleasure — and it may be one of severe conflict and death to me. Not my will, but thine O God, be done. If it is necessary that I should fall on the battlefield for my country, I am ready. I have no misgivings about, or lack of confidence in, the cause in which I am engaged, and my courage does not halt or falter. I know how strongly American Civilization now leans upon the triumph of the Government, and how great a debt we owe to those who went before us through the blood and   suffering of the Revolution. And I am willing — perfectly willing — to lay down all my joys in this life, to help maintain this Government, and to pay that debt.

But, my dear wife, when I know that with my own joys I lay down nearly all of yours, and replace them in this life with cares and sorrows — when, after having eaten for long years the bitter fruit of orphanage myself, I must offer it as their only sustenance to my dear little children — is it weak or dishonorable, while the banner of my purpose floats calmly and proudly in the breeze, that my unbounded love for you, my darling wife and children, should struggle in fierce, though useless, contest with my love of country.

Sarah, my love for you is deathless, it seems to bind me to you with mighty cables that nothing but Omnipotence could break; and yet my love of Country comes over me like a strong wind and bears me irresistibly on with all these chains to the battlefield.

The memories of the blissful moments I have spent with you come creeping over me, and I feel most gratified to God and to you that I have enjoyed them so long. And hard it is for me to give them up and burn to ashes the hopes of future years, when God willing, we might still have lived and loved together and seen our sons grow up to honorable manhood around us. I have, I know, but few and small claims upon Divine Providence, but something whispers to me—perhaps it is the wafted prayer of my little Edgar—that I shall return to my loved ones unharmed. If I do not, my dear Sarah, never forget how much I love you, and when my last breath escapes me on the battlefield, it will whisper your name.

Forgive my many faults, and the many pains I have caused you. How thoughtless and foolish I have often been! How gladly would I wash out with my tears every little spot upon your happiness, and struggle with all the misfortune of this world, to shield you and my children from harm. But I cannot. I must watch you from the spirit land and hover near you, while you buffet the storms with your precious little freight, and wait with sad patience till we meet to part no more.

But, O Sarah! If the dead can come back to this earth and flit unseen around those they loved, I shall always be near you; in the brightest day and in the darkest night—amidst your happiest scenes and gloomiest hours—always, always; and if there be a soft breeze upon your cheek, it shall be my breath; or the cool air fans your throbbing temple, it shall be my spirit passing by.

and if there be a soft breeze upon your cheek, it shall be my breath; or the cool air fans your throbbing temple, it shall be my spirit passing by.

Sarah, do not mourn me dead; think I am gone and wait for thee, for we shall meet again.

As for my little boys, they will grow as I have done, and never know a father's love and care. Little Willie is too young to remember me long, and my blue-eyed Edgar will keep my frolics with him among the dimmest memories of his childhood. Sarah, I have unlimited confidence in your maternal care and your development of their characters. Tell my two mothers his and hers I call God's blessing upon them. O Sarah, I wait for you there! Come to me, and lead thither my children.

Sullivan

1. Sullivan recognized several Timeless feminine attributes in his wife. Can you name some of them?

2. Which Timeless principles that you have learned can you practice most to create your own lifelong love affair like Sullivan and Sarah had?

Summary

Congratulations! You have reached the end of your Fascinating Womanhood for the Timeless Woman study. You are now equipped with the information you need to improve your relationships and to fascinate everyone you meet. Remember to revisit Timeless often, as well as your valuable notes in this workbook.

Before you go...

What is something that you learned in your study with this workbook that surprised you about yourself?

What have you learned that will make a difference to your future relationships?